# THREE
## of a
# KIND

## The Allen Carrington Spalding Trio

Written by Terri Lyne Carrington
Illustrations by Ramsess

AuthorHouse™
1663 Liberty Drive
Bloomington, IN 47403
www.authorhouse.com
Phone: 833-262-8899

Because of the dynamic nature of the Internet, any web addresses or links contained in
this book may have changed since publication and may no longer be valid. The views
expressed in this work are solely those of the author and do not necessarily reflect the views
of the publisher, and the publisher hereby disclaims any responsibility for them.

This book is printed on acid-free paper.

ISBN: 978-1-6655-7059-6 (sc)
ISBN: 978-1-6655-7060-2 (e)

Library of Congress Control Number: 2022916871

Print information available on the last page.

Published by AuthorHouse  03/17/2023

authorHOUSE®

In memory of Geri Allen

This non-fiction, illustrated poem is about three women who became musical companions through their love of jazz. Geri Allen, Terri Lyne Carrington, and esperanza spalding toured the world, sharing their love for each other and their listeners, while igniting imaginations and challenging perceptions of gender roles in their beloved art form. This poem is written and illustrated in the spirit of encouraging young girls from all over to play instruments and dream big.

This is a story about one, two, three of a kind,

an extraordinary jazz trio whose tones were divine.

A little girl from Boston, who played drums with Dizzy and all the greats,

met a "bad" young pianist from Detroit, whose style was playful and ornate.

The two performed with Ella's bassist, Mr. Betts, at the jazz club, *One Step Down.*

Upon playing, they knew it was special, as they struck a most harmonious sound.

Sometime later, a virtuoso was born in the hills of Portland, Oregon.

She started on violin, then continued with bass, and soon began to sing her own song.

Each had formal training and went to college to learn composition and music theory.

But their most valuable lessons took place in the jazz capital of the world, at the jam sessions in New York City.

Taking a bite out of the Big Apple was difficult at times, yet necessary for "cutting one's teeth."

But they knew to never give up on the career they loved, to persevere, and not skip a beat.

The pianist and the drummer waited nearly 20 years for the bassist to arrive.

And once they heard her, they knew their melodies would soar and their circle would thrive.

The three didn't really question why it seemed they were an anomaly.

Though they sometimes asked themselves, "Why aren't there more girls like me?"

It seemed mostly boys played these instruments, with few women as role models or peers.

But eventually, stereotypes began to fade, as listeners closed their eyes and opened their ears.

They shared the role of the rhythm section, to support, compliment, and inspire,

while always pushing each other further, especially when playing Geri's song, "Feed the Fire."

They loved to come together on the small stage at the world-famous Village Vanguard,

where the lights are dim, the tables close, and the fans cheer with warm regard.

A new feeling emerged for them, and they could finally be their authentic selves.

This sparked an unusual question, "Is there a woman's aesthetic in jazz that can be heard or felt?"

Without being afraid to make mistakes, and with the freedom to create one's own interesting stories,

the music itself has much more potential, and gender balance keeps it from being boring!

Each composed and arranged for their own bands, and had solo careers that were a whopping success.

But they never forgot the thrill of playing together, so when they reunited it was the best.

To be three in body and one in spirit was an unspoken, yet essential goal.

And with trust, compassion, and intense listening, together they could reach for places unknown.

For six years Geri, Terri and esperanza joined forces, unlocking their own potential and entangling their imaginations for audiences, young and old.

They reconstructed "standards," administered unconditional love, and helped to bring about a paradigm shift – as the incomparable ACS trio.

# GLOSSARY/LEARNING GUIDE

## Words

**administered**–showed, provided, or applied something

**aesthetic**–a set of creative, expressive, and cultural principles that can guide the work of a particular artist, artistic style, era, and/or movement

**anomaly**-something that is out of the ordinary or does not fit in with the mainstream or majority

**arranged**–changing a composition by another musician to fit for a different group of players; a remix or different version of an original composition

**Big Apple** - a nickname for New York City

**club**–a restaurant or communal place where people go to socialize and hear music

**compassion**-great care, devotion, or love for something/someone

**composition**–a piece of music written by a musician (often called a composer)

**"cutting one's teeth"**–acquire initial practice or experience of a particular sphere of activity or with a particular organization

**distinctive**–special; unlike anything or anyone else

**entangling**–causing two or more distinct things to get intertwined together

**essential**–something that is absolutely necessary

**extraordinary**-very special, different, not normal

**gender**–a range of characteristics pertaining to a vast spectrum including, but not limited to femininity and masculinity and differentiating between them

**goal**–something that one is reaching for or aiming to achieve

**harmonious** — sounding good together while playing different parts/melodies

**incomparable**–unable to be compared to anyone or anything else, at a higher level than most.

**jam session** — an event at which musicians come together to play, meet each other, and experiment with new musical ideas in a communal setting

**jazz** — a unique style of music of Black American origin, characterized by improvisation, syncopation, and rhythms, all of which can shift throughout a song; traditionally includes brass and woodwind instruments, drums, piano, bass, and guitar.

**melodies** — plural of melody, i.e., the main idea or theme of a song; the pattern of pitches and rhythm that creates a tune or song, most often played by the lead vocalists or instrumentalists

**music theory** — a study of the practices of music; a way of thinking about and analyzing music, often taught in music school

**ornate**–detailed, with many different parts/patterns.

**paradigm**–a way of thinking about a concept or topic

**peers** — people who are at your same level or stage of life

**persevere** — to keep going or continue towards something, against all odds or obstacles

**potential**–the possibility to become something more or greater

**reconstructed** — made new again or changed in a way that reinvents

**rhythm section** — the section of the band that keeps the foundation of the song going throughout, usually including bass, drums, piano, and/or guitar

**role model**–a person one admires, respects, and may want to be like one day

**standard** — a musical composition that is an important part of repertoire, widely known and performed by jazz musicians

**stereotype**–a belief that many people hold about a particular group or type of people that is often untrue

**trio**–a group of three people

**vigorous**–with intense feeling or strength

**virtuoso**–a musician with exceptionally great technical skills on their instrument


## People

**Geri Allen** (1957-2017) was a world-renowned jazz pianist, composer, educator, and ethnomusicologist. She was exemplary in her life and career and set high standards for a variety of modern jazz styles while maintaining her own incomparable, distinctive expression and voice in music.

**Keter Betts** (1928-2005) was a jazz bassist originally from Port Chester, New York, who later became an important part of the Washington, D.C. jazz community. He was best known for playing with Ella Fitzgerald, but also played with Dinah Washington, Bobby Timmons, and many others.

**Terri Lyne Carrington** (1965-present) is a GRAMMY Award-winning drummer, composer, and producer, noted for her activism and advocacy in jazz and jazz education. As a visionary, she founded the Berklee Institute of Jazz and Gender Justice to raise the voices of women and non-binary jazz artists and to bring awareness to the inequities they face.

**Ella Fitzgerald** (1917-1996) was a legendary vocalist known as the "First Lady of Jazz" and was notable for her horn-like approach to improvising. Fitzgerald's voice and career made such an impact on jazz, music history, and American culture that she continues to be celebrated and honored to this day throughout the world.

**Dizzy Gillespie** (1917-1993) was a prominent trumpet player, composer, and bandleader, known for pioneering bebop along with Charlie Parker and for exploring the connection between jazz and Afro-Cuban music.

**Ramsess** (1956-present) is a multimedia artist and curator from Los Angeles, California, who has been active for over four decades. Ramsess specializes in drawings, paintings, sculptures, stained-glass windows, mosaics, and textiles, many of which showcase jazz music and other aspects of Black culture and aesthetics.

**esperanza spalding** (1984 to present) is a GRAMMY Award-winning bassist, composer, vocalist, and educator, who is known to be stylistically expansive, ever-evolving, and forward-thinking in her artistic approach. In 2017, she was appointed professor of the Practice of Music at Harvard University.

Thanks and acknowledgement to esperanza spalding, Mount Allen, Terry Stewart, Aja Burrell Wood, Devon Gates, Sarah Godcher Murphy, Oliver Ragsdale, and to Ramsess for contributing such beautiful illustrations.

Printed in the United States
by Baker & Taylor Publisher Services